Rain

by Erin Edison
Consulting Editor: Gail Saunders-Smith, PhD

CAPSTONE PRESS
a capstone imprint

Pebble Plus is published by Capstone Press,
1710 Roe Crest Drive, North Mankato, Minnesota 56003.
www.capstonepub.com

Copyright © 2012 by Capstone Press, a Capstone imprint. All rights reserved.
No part of this publication may be reproduced in whole or in part, or stored in a retrieval system, or transmitted in any form or by any means, electronic, mechanical, photocopying, recording, or otherwise, without written permission of the publisher. For information regarding permission, write to Capstone Press,
1710 Roe Crest Drive, North Mankato, Minnesota 56003.

Library of Congress Cataloging-in-Publication Data
Edison, Erin.
  Rain / by Erin Edison.
      p. cm.—(Pebble plus. Weather basics)
  Summary: "Simple text and full-color photographs describe rain and its role in the water cycle"—Provided by publisher.
  Includes bibliographical references and index.
  ISBN 978-1-4296-6055-6 (library binding)
  ISBN 978-1-4296-7079-1 (paperback)
  ISBN 978-1-4296-8752-2 (saddle-stitch)
  1. Rain and rainfall—Juvenile literature. 2. Hydrologic cycle—Juvenile literature. I. Title. II. Series.
  QC924.7.E35 2012
  551.57'7—dc22   2010053973

Editorial Credits
Erika L. Shores, editor; Kyle Grenz, designer; Laura Manthe, production specialist

Photo Credits
Alamy: C.O. Mercial, 21, Dave Chapman, 13; Getty Images Inc.: Tim Boyle, 17; Shutterstock: Andrew Chin, cover, Attila Huszti, 1, Claudio Rossol, 11, dpaint, 7, dutourdumonde, 15, Marcelo Dufflocq W., 5, Mona Makela, back cover, Nixx Photography, 19, SebStock, 9

Artistic Effects
Shutterstock: marcus55

Capstone Press thanks Mike Shores, earth science teacher at RBA Public Charter School in Mankato, Minnesota, for his assistance on this book.

Note to Parents and Teachers

The Weather Basics series supports national science standards related to earth science. This book describes and illustrates rain. The images support early readers in understanding the text. The repetition of words and phrases helps early readers learn new words. This book also introduces early readers to subject-specific vocabulary words, which are defined in the Glossary section. Early readers may need assistance to read some words and to use the Table of Contents, Glossary, Read More, Internet Sites, and Index sections of the book.

Table of Contents

What Is Rain?.......... 4
The Water Cycle 8
Floods and Droughts ...16

Glossary..................22
Read More 23
Internet Sites............23
Index.....................24

What Is Rain?

Rain is water that falls

from clouds.

It helps plants grow.

It makes puddles.

Rain brings water to living things. Rain fills lakes where fish live.
Plants use water in the ground.

The Water Cycle

Rain starts as water on the ground. Water in lakes and oceans evaporates. Water vapor rises into the sky.

In the air, water vapor cools.

It turns into liquid droplets.

This is called condensation.

Droplets stick to tiny particles in the air. Then clouds form.

Droplets in the clouds grow and become heavier than air. Rain falls. This process is called precipitation.

13

Evaporation, condensation, and precipitation are the water cycle's three parts. Water evaporates, makes clouds, then falls to the ground. This pattern happens again and again.

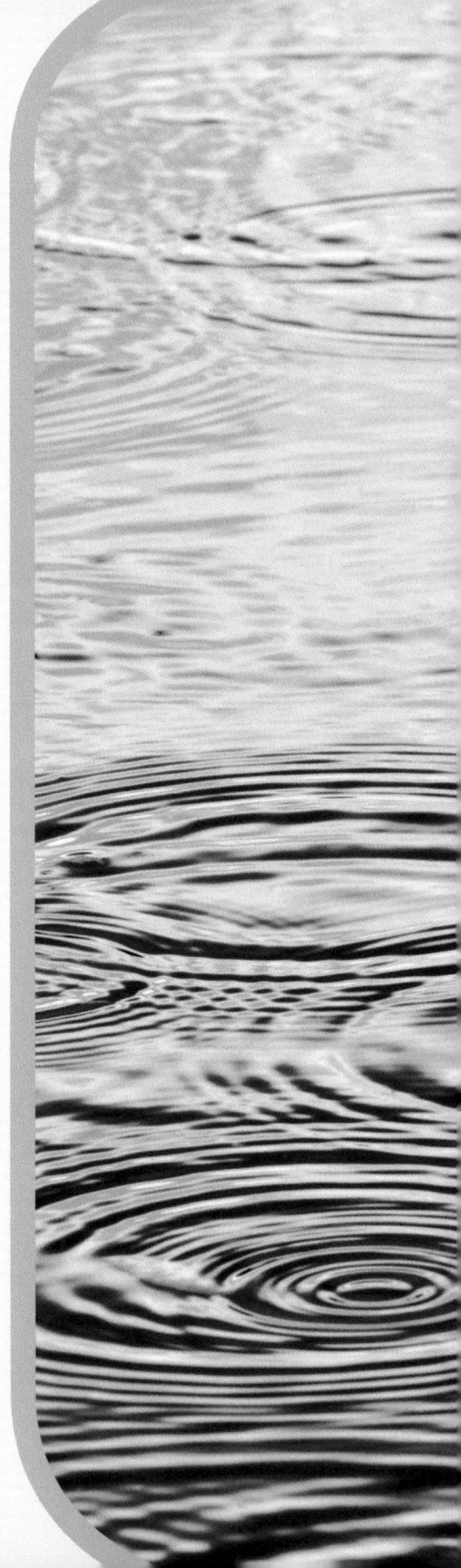

Floods and Droughts

When too much rain falls, water covers places it normally doesn't. This is called a flood. Floods damage roads, crops, and buildings.

Droughts happen when too little rain falls. Rivers and lakes dry up. Soil becomes hard. Plants and animals die without water.

Too much or too little rain can hurt living things. Animals, people, and plants need just enough rain.

Glossary

condensation—the act of turning from a gas into a liquid

crop—a plant grown in large amounts; crops usually are grown for food

drought—a long period of weather with little or no rainfall

evaporate—the action of a liquid changing into a gas; heat causes water to evaporate

flood—to overflow with water

particle—a tiny piece of something; water droplets stick to dust, salt, and other tiny particles in the air to form clouds

water vapor—water in the form of a gas; water vapor is made of tiny bits of water that cannot be seen

Read More

Goldsmith, Mike. *The Weather.* Now We Know About. New York: Crabtree Pub., 2010.

Higginson, Sheila Sweeny. *Drip, Drop! The Rain Won't Stop!* Your Turn, My Turn Reader. New York: Simon Spotlight, 2010.

Salas, Laura Purdie. *Colors of Weather.* Colors All Around. Mankato, Minn.: Capstone Press, 2011.

Internet Sites

FactHound offers a safe, fun way to find Internet sites related to this book. All of the sites on FactHound have been researched by our staff.

Here's all you do:

Visit www.facthound.com

Type in this code: 9781429660556

Check out projects, games and lots more at www.capstonekids.com

Index

animals, 6, 18, 20
clouds, 4, 10, 12, 14
condensation, 10, 14
crops, 16
droplets, 10, 12
droughts, 18
evaporation, 8, 14
floods, 16

lakes, 6, 8, 18
oceans, 8
plants, 4, 6, 18, 20
puddles, 4
rivers, 18
water cycle, 14
water vapor, 8, 10

Word Count: 180
Grade: 1
Early-Intervention Level: 18